MERLIN AND THE WOODS OF TIME

T0347773

for Alex Clifton, Cestrian

Dramatis Personae

THE WOOD

WATERCUP
an itinerant healer

LILY
his best friend and helper

ELAINE
the Lady of The Woods

CAMELOT

KING ARTHUR

QUEEN GUINEVERE

SIR LANCELOT

SIR GAWAIN
and

SIR MORDRED
Knights

SIR LUCAN
and

SIR BORS
former Knights, now Experts

HERALD
a singer

MERLIN

THE WHITE KNIGHT

MRS GORMAN
a service professional

NOTE ON LILY

Lily communicates in two ways, indicated by typography:

1. She mimes, <u>and other characters interpret aloud what she means.</u>

2. Or she mimes and simultaneously speaks the line in Welsh, as printed.

Merlin and the Woods of Time was first performed on July 14th 2011 in Grosvenor Park, Chester, as part of the open-air summer season produced by Chester Performs. The play was staged in repertory with *As You Like It* by William Shakespeare.

Directed by Alex Clifton
Designed by takis
Music composed by David Shrubsole
Casting by Kay Magson

Watercup, **DAVID HARTLEY**
Lily, **REBECCA SMITH WILLIAMS**
Elaine, **ROSIE JONES**
Arthur, **SEVAN STEPHAN**
Guinevere, **SOPHIE ROBERTS**
Lancelot, **PAUL-RYAN CARBERRY**
Gawain, **MIKE BURNSIDE**
Mordred, **ROBERT MOUNTFORD**
Lucan, **ANDREW WESTFIELD**
Bors, **NICK ASBURY**
Herald, **DAVID RICARDO-PEARCE**
Merlin, **ALAN MCMAHON**
The White Knight, **ROB COMPTON**
Mrs Gorman, **NATALIE GRADY**
Musician, **TAREK MERCHANT**

With thanks to Rebecca Smith Williams
and Angharad Fflur Dafydd for the mystical wood-warble.

ACT ONE

HERALD: *Once in the woods of a world you know*
            A story grew where the lime-trees grow
            And it grew till you sat where you sit right now
            Between a first word and a final bow
            And when it was over, I heard it cry
            'Why are we stopping?' Don't ask me why…

WATERCUP and LILY. WATERCUP sits, exhausted. LILY signs to him.

WATERCUP: <u>Why are we stopping</u>…Don't ask me why,
            Lily, I can't walk any more, we've walked
            since doomsday afternoon is what it feels like.
            <u>How can we eat if we stop</u>…<u>We have no food,
            no money…</u> I *know* we need
            <u>a place of many people</u>, I *know* we need
            a crowd to sell our medicines to, I *know*
            you're hungry, but I'm starving! I'm fading…
            illusions of some great celestial picnic
            swim before my eyes… Lily, I fear
            we've come to the very heart of the wild north-west,
            a place of ghosts and vagabonds, outcasts
            staring vacantly ahead, I seem to…
            see them in my dreams…

LILY: Ni'n mynd y ffordd anghywir,
            ni angen mynd y ffordd na! [1]

WATERCUP: Now you make your sad
            nonsensical word-music…

LILY: Cymraeg fi'n
            siarad, ffwl! [2]

---

[1]   We're going the wrong way,
       we need to go that way!

[2]   I'm speaking Welsh, you fool!

WATERCUP: Stay with me, poor Lily,
be not lost to madness…

LILY: O Iesu Grist… [3]

WATERCUP: I fear the lamp of reason dims, for I seem
to hear love's music carried on the breeze…

We hear the voice of ELAINE.

ELAINE: *The woods are wide, Sir Dum-de-dum*
The path is only narrow,
Still I abide, Sir Dum-de-dum
In my abiding sorrow…

WATERCUP: Oh Lily, are we dreaming?

ELAINE comes, oblivious to them, reading a poem from her commonplace-book.

ELAINE: *The woods are big, Sir Dum-de-dum*
And I am only little,
But yet I love, Sir Dum-de-dum
Without any…requittle. No…
I whistle like a kettle? No!

WATERCUP: *And Love rides into battle?*

ELAINE: Who are you? Help!
Woodland folk! Somebody help!

WATERCUP: O Lady
Poetical, in your most leafy beauty,
a-walking in your lovely bower – I mean
leafy bower and lovely beauty –

ELAINE: A troll!
A troll in the wood! In human form, a troll!
I am in distress! I need a Knight!

WATERCUP: May your most
holy pardon be most wholly begged
by your humble servant.

[3]   Oh Jesus Christ…

ELAINE:	This troll has mastered English.
	He has a familiar! *(To LILY.)* Were you once a cat?
	Can he change you back?
WATERCUP:	This is my sister, Lily.
	She's not my sister but she's like a sister.
	I've known her since the day I found myself
	abandoned on the forest trail.
ELAINE:	Do I look
	as if I care? Why can't she speak?
WATERCUP:	Her mind
	is gone, she has no words.
LILY:	Fi'n dod o Gymru,
	y twpsyn! [4]
WATERCUP:	She makes those lovely sounds
	as if they had a meaning, it's some secret
	language of the dell perhaps, a tongue
	known only to the cuckoos.
ELAINE:	Or the trolls!
	Is she putting a spell on me?
WATERCUP:	(Lily!) We're not
	trolls, we are travellers. Your exquisite poem,
	lady, was most pleasing to the ear.
	I have heard of many knights and their noble exploits
	in love and battle, but Sir – Dum-de-dum –
	is not a name I know. Do you mean Sir Dum
	of Dum?
ELAINE:	Fool, I am destined –
	as I know from a dream I have, a dream in which
	a golden book falls open to reveal
	a name so bright I have to shield my eyes –
	where was I?
WATERCUP:	Destined.

[4]   I come from Wales, you idiot!

ELAINE: Destined yes, I am destined
              to be the lady of a gallant Knight
              whose name is of three parts, so, 'dum-de-dum'
              I write for now. One day I will fill that space
              with the noble name of my love, but – what is she saying?

LILY is pointing her fingers down her throat.

WATERCUP: Well, she's – saying how very sorry she is
              that God has struck her dumb, for, otherwise,
              she'd cry your loveliness throughout the world.
ELAINE: Hm. Why does she lift two fingers?
WATERCUP: That's to tell me –
              she wishes you and she – were close as sisters.
ELAINE: I'm sure she does but it probably won't happen.
              She being a troll of the woods and I a lady.
WATERCUP: (Lily, stop.)
ELAINE: I have no time for this!
              I am bound for the Chapel of Sir Groevanor,
              hard by which Chapel I shall see the Knights
              of Camelot contest the Champion's Shield!
              And there, my dreams inform me,
              will my true love be triumphant.
WATERCUP: I – too am bound for the Chapel of – that place
              you said, I too shall enter the glorious Lists
              for the glory of – my cause.
ELAINE: What cause is that then?
WATERCUP: A noble cause! I shall mount my steed –
ELAINE: Where's he then?
WATERCUP: He, um – feedeth in the forest.
ELAINE: You're not a Knight!
              You look like the weedy boy who makes the shoes
              for the weedy man who stoops to take the heel
              of the weediest Knight to mount his weedy horse.
              By which I mean you're nobody.
WATERCUP: I'm nobody
              you know.

ELAINE: I know the names
                of all the gallant Knights. What's your name?

WATERCUP: My name?

ELAINE: Sir Nobody.

WATERCUP: No, no –

ELAINE: Sir Bootsole.

WATERCUP: No!

ELAINE: Sir Wipe-the-Stable-Clean.

WATERCUP: I am
                the Knight – the Knight of…the Tree.

ELAINE: The Knight of the Tree. Which tree.

WATERCUP: That one.

ELAINE: That one.
                What, do you live in that tree.

WATERCUP: I pledge *allegiance*
                to it.

ELAINE: You pledge allegiance to that tree.

WATERCUP: To the tree, the wood, to all things in nature,
                the hills and dales, the winter mist, the summer skies,
                the birds, bees, butterflies, the, er, the badgers.

ELAINE: You pledge allegiance to the badgers.

WATERCUP: All things!
                From the eagle lofty on his – lofty bough,
                down to the meanest ant or earthworm.

ELAINE: Eeuw.

WATERCUP: I am the Knight of All Things God made.

ELAINE: So you couldn't find a Lady to be Knight of.

WATERCUP: No. Well not till now.

ELAINE: Not till now?
                What's *now* got that *back then* didn't have?
                Has something stopped the world while we weren't looking?
                You have no Lady, and you are no Knight.
                It's all so sad it's funny, then in fact
                so funny it's sad again. Well I leave you, troll,
                and your ginger cat you turned to a ginger fool,

>   and your noble steed invisible,
>   and your best friends the weeds. I bid you good day.

ELAINE leaves. WATERCUP enthralled.

WATERCUP: Good day…good day…So is the sun a firefly.
So is the sea a teardrop. Good day?
Can ever voice have understated so?
Good day – the day against which all my days
are leaves that fall, by other leaves concealed!

LILY: Dilyna hi! [5]

WATERCUP: Good day – the – what do you mean?

LILY: Mae'n gwybod y ffordd, mae'n mynd lle ma na bobol!
Twrnament! Allwn ni weithio na a neud arian! [6]

WATERCUP: *Go after her!* Of course! Follow my heart!
O sister, in your simple way, you too
point me to my destiny! A good day?
A day that *lasts* for good, that lasts forever!
To the Chapel of Sir Groevanor!

WATERCUP strides off after Elaine. LILY follows with all their things. Music. Processional. The COURT OF CAMELOT arrives: a HERALD with the Champion's Shield; KING ARTHUR and QUEEN GUINEVERE; SIR LANCELOT, SIR GAWAIN and SIR MORDRED; SIR LUCAN and SIR BORS, bearing the great yellow book WISDOM'S ALMANACK; ELAINE, and ATTENDANTS. They pass through to the Tournament behind. WATERCUP and LILY arrive in time to see the end of the Procession. LUCAN and BORS take up position in the 'puppet tent'. Slits in the back allow them to watch the Lists, before turning to replay the action to us.

LUCAN: Welcome, riff-raff of the Realm of Arthur,
to the Chapel of Sir Groevanor, for the Great
Tournament of the Champions' Shield. Now it's true

[5]   Follow her!

[6]   She knows the way, she's going where there's people.
        A tournament! We can work there and make money!

22

we all have to tighten our belts – we don't but *you* do –
so you can't afford a ringside seat like *we* can,
but this is the next best thing, the very latest
in bringing the action home. These thrilling jousts
by the use of cutting-edge hand-puppetry,
will be broadly cast by us to you. You are watching…

BORS: Sir Lucan!

LUCAN: Lucan for *Love*…
Sir Bors!

BORS: Bors for England.

LUCAN: Lucan for Love and Bors for England. Bors,
talk us through the morning.

BORS: Thank you, Lucan.
Three bouts this morning, Tilting With The Lance.
Sir Lancelot of the Lake is in the lists,
we'll see Gawain, and Mordred is a starter.
The going is soft-to-gullible, it would favour
chargers over cold-bloods. Lancelot
has got to be in with a shout, having despatched
Sir Percival in the joust-a-plaisance
at York on Whitsuntide.

LUCAN: You could cut the air
with a knife at the end of the day.

BORS: Very much so.
Let's look at the form-book, Lucan.

LUCAN: Go for it, Bors.

*BORS looks in WISDOM'S ALMANACK; LUCAN looks out at the Lists. LILY
is doing all the work setting up their stall, while WATERCUP paces about.*

WATERCUP: *Good day, good day*, did you hear she bade me *good day*?
Then I saw her in the procession, did you see there,
she beamed right at me, Lily! What are you saying?
<u>I think – that tree – just winked at me</u>… stop it Lily!
I mean it – look, a four-leaf clover! Fortune
favours me! But this will reveal her heart!

She loves me…She loves me not…
oh heavens, the suspense…she…oh.
Stupid folklore. Why would you believe that?

LUCAN sees WATERCUP pouring out cups of water.

LUCAN:　　Oi, peasant, fetch us a water cup!

WATERCUP:　　　On its way, sir,
but my name is actually –

LUCAN:　　　　A water cup, I'm thirsty!

ELAINE arrives, on her way to the Ladies' Convenience.

ELAINE:　　Watercup? Is your name *Watercup*?

WATERCUP: No he *asked* for a water cup, my name –

LUCAN: *(To ELAINE.)* Hello sweetheart,
you can serve me any time…

ELAINE: *(To WATERCUP.)* This is your job?
You run around and pour out cups of water.
Cups of water – *Watercup*! That's amazing,
your name's just like your job!

WATERCUP: *(Serving LUCAN.)* No, let me explain –

ELAINE:　　You pour out water, near to a ladies' toilet.
For the birds and bees and badgers! This is so funny.

WATERCUP: I am a healer, actually, and I serve
cooling drinks to the knights.

LUCAN:　　　Enough water, lad,
fetch us a jug of wine!

WATERCUP:　　Yes, sir.

LUCAN: *(To ELAINE.)*　　D'you fancy
a stiffener, sweetheart? Think we've met before…

BORS:　　Here come the Knights, Sir Lucan!

LUCAN turns his attention to the Lists, as WATERCUP serves him and BORS.

ELAINE:　　Watercup, who fetches cups of water.

WATERCUP: At least my name has three parts. Dum-de-dum.

ELAINE:　　That may be so but it's not *Sir* Watercup,
is it?

WATERCUP: It shall be some day.

ELAINE: Shall it really.

WATERCUP: Watercup was I named on the day I met you.
Watercup shall I be.

ELAINE: How interesting.

WATERCUP: One day you shall see me fight in a noble cause
against impossible odds, and for a lady.

ELAINE: Some lady who's in want of a cup of water?
I'm not. I'm not in want of a Knight at all.
I have found one. I saw him from afar.
His standard is of azure-blue and his name
is of three parts. As is his character,
for he is brave, sweet, honourable, and – four parts.
Noble, honourable, handsome, brave – five parts.
Handsome, noble, sweet – oh the joust is starting!

A drum-roll, and ELAINE runs out. WATERCUP notices Wisdom's Almanack.

WATERCUP: She has found her Knight? Then I have found my night-time.
Still, hope grows where nothing grows. What *is* this
book they treat like treasure…
'Wisdom's Almanack…The Guide Compleat
to Chivalry, Its Codes and Exemplars…
Once, on the Field of Claverton, Sir Wimbold
in the sable colours of the Lady Belgrave
hath Tempered the Sword of Justice three times
with Humanity and Mercy… At Yuletide
on the Field of Christleton, Sir Mickle Trafford
Hath righteously defended the Good Name
Of Lady Hoole, Lady Wervin, Lady Foregate,
and Lady Chorlton-by-Backford', oh, sweet ladies,
noble Sir Mickle Trafford! *(He daydreams.)* In August,
on the field of – Groevanor, Sir Watercup
hath rode in the colours of the Lady – what?
I don't know her name!

LILY: Der ma a blydi helpa fi! [7]

WATERCUP puts the book down and goes back to the stall.

WATERCUP: Sorry, Lily, you're right, we have our work,
we brew, we serve, we heal, and so we live.
For sure, in this Almanack you'll read no record
of Sir Watercup. But I wonder…if I read that,
then I would know what *they* know…

A trumpet sounds.

LUCAN: And we're off!
Gawain in green, Mordred in jet-black…
Gawain is riding Winalot, his warmblood
charger, while Sir Mordred's on No-Hoper…
Gawain is aiming high, Mordred low,
it's going to be one or the other, that's jousting,
and bang and Mordred's off, he's down, Gawain
has taken it, wham-bam, that'll do nicely,
blood on the grass, we like it there, goodnight
and so to Bedivere. I'm Lucan for Love.

BORS: And I'm Bors for England. Lancelot's next up.

WATERCUP: Lily, I have got to get that book.
I *know* the disgusting man and the boring man
are using it, but look it's so gigantic
it must be the only copy on God's earth.
And it could turn me to the Knight I know
I'm destined to become!

HERALD: A water cup!

MORDRED comes, covered in blood, supported by the HERALD. LILY assesses his injuries and signs to WATERCUP.

WATERCUP: Ruptured spleen, cracked rib, internal bleeding,
indigestion, scurvy, halitosis,
earache, anger issues…That's a florin.

[7]   Come here and bloody help me!

MORDRED pays. LILY and WATERCUP help him into their tent

LUCAN: Hey Bors, you know a little bird just told me
the Passage-of-Arms is to be judged today
by Queen Guinevere.

BORS: That's a first in jousting,
Lucan, that's extraordinary.

LUCAN: A *lady*
judging on the tilts? Do me a favour.
How can she know the rule on strikes?

BORS: Chivalric
correctness gone mad. I'm Bors for England.

LUCAN: I'm Lucan for Love. Now, don't get me wrong,
that Guinevere can judge me on *my* tilts
any time she likes, eh…

BORS: That's a good one.
That's a good use of humour.

They go to the Convenience. WATERCUP emerges from the healing tent.

WATERCUP: Look, they're taking a break, this is my chance…
Lily, bandage him up, it's now or never!

He runs to the puppet tent, lifts up the Almanack, stuffs it under his shirt and creeps back to the healing tent, from which MORDRED emerges.

WATERCUP: How are you feeling, sir?

MORDRED: Ninety-seven
jousts. Ninety-six defeats. One draw.
Get in there! I shall build on that. One day
God willing I shall draw again. On that day
Camelot shall know the name of…Mordred.

WATERCUP: I think they know your name. You're the one who
always loses.

MORDRED: Wrong. Not always. Once, in Lincoln,
I fell from my horse, but…*so did my opponent.*
It had never happened before, but…now it's happened.
D'you see? D'you see the pattern?

MORDRED goes. LILY emerges. LUCAN and BORS return to their tent.

WATERCUP: *(To LILY.)* Go round, creep about, find out the lady's name.
<u>What am *I* going to do</u>? Read this book.

LILY goes. The trumpet sounds. BORS watches the joust, LUCAN relays it.

BORS: Off they go, the second bout of the morning,
and for those of you watching this in sable-and-argent,
Gawain's in vert, Lancelot's in azure
and bang!

LUCAN: That's got to hurt.

BORS: Gawain is off!

LUCAN: Wham-bam-Bedivere, blood on the grass,
that's jousting! There's a lady in the stands
swooning with emotion, look she's down,
it's another conquest for Sir Lancelot!

BORS: And *that* is very much your department,
the ladies, very much a colourful
sideshow to the action.

LUCAN: That was her,
thought I knew her, the Lady of The Woods…
Looks like she's got the hots for Lancelot.
That's not going to please the Queen eh, Bors?

BORS: Indeed.
– Why's that?

LUCAN: Why's that? The Queen and Lancelot?
You spent the last few months alone in a cave?

BORS: Er, yes, I did.

LUCAN: The Lady of The Woods, eh…
What *is* that lady's name?

LILY has come back and is signing letters for WATERCUP.

WATERCUP: <u>Egg</u> – E, <u>Lip</u> – L, <u>Arse</u> – A, <u>Eye</u> – I,
<u>Nose</u> – N, <u>Elbow</u> – E. That's her name? –
Arseline? Go back a bit. Eglaine?
Eglantine? Elaine! Elaine! What else?

She <u>threw</u> – she threw her <u>favour</u>…for me?
No no, what am I thinking, for one of the knights,
the – <u>long knight</u>, long, oh <u>a long lance</u>,
Sir Lance – <u>a bit? A lot!</u> Sir Lance-a-lot?
<u>She threw…her favour to Sir Lancelot.</u> Oh.

Poor WATERCUP. The HERALD drags in GAWAIN.

HERALD:	We need a water cup!
WATERCUP:	That's me!
HERALD:	Gawain.
GAWAIN:	Blast ye Lancelot, yer silver-tongued slim-waisted cool bilingual metrosexual fairy!

LILY assesses him and signals, WATERCUP makes notes.

WATERCUP: <u>Burst liver, ruptured kidneys,</u>
<u>lance envy</u> (lance envy? that's a new one),
<u>lumbago, runny nose.</u> That's three florins.

The HERALD finds some coins on GAWAIN and pays. They drag him into the healing tent. The HERALD departs. WATERCUP goes back to the Almanack.

WATERCUP:	You do it, Lily, I'm busy.
LILY:	Darllen llyfr? [8]
WATERCUP:	Yes reading a book, a book that could change our lives!
LILY:	Bu ti byth yn farchog! [9]
WATERCUP:	I *will* be a knight, I'll best all-comers and win my lady's hand! One day I shall fight for her in a noble cause!
LILY:	Anghofia'r fenyw dwp! [10]
WATERCUP:	I *can't* forget the stupid la – she's not a stupid lady!

[8]   Reading a book?

[9]   You'll never be a knight!

[10]   Forget the stupid lady!

She is the Lady Elaine. And I can't forget her.

What do you mean I'm reading it upside-down?

How would you know, you can't even read the words.

LILY: Diw e ddim yn gymraeg! [11]

WATERCUP: Your mystical wood-warble...

O, my love for Elaine makes all sounds
melodious.

GAWAIN: Get yer ragged arse in here,

yer parasitic paramedic vulture!

*LILY goes back in. WATERCUP slowly turns the Almanack upside down, as
LUCAN and BORS realise it's missing.*

LUCAN: Aye-aye, where's Wisdom gone? That yellow tome

we always heave about to look important.

BORS: It was right there on the plinth.

LUCAN: Well who cares.

I never read it anyway.

BORS: Nor me.

I know it off by heart, like you.

LUCAN: Like me?

Books, old lad? Books are for girls. Chin-chin.

They drink. Drum-roll at the Tournament. WATERCUP gazes at the pictures.

WATERCUP: Mysterious sketches scribbled in the margins...

portending what? Ingredients
for a liquid red in colour...but this picture
shows the sun at dawn and then at twilight...
then all four seasons side-by-side, and stars
that fly away like birds...what *is* this potion?
And here's another, elements of a compound
blue in colour. Here though, in these pictures
the sun sits in the selfsame place...*always*...

[11]   It's not in Welsh!

The trumpet sounds.

LUCAN: We're off, to the left in black on his dark horse
             the dark horse, the underdog, Mordred,
             against the azure blue of the ladies' choice
             Sir Lancelot of the Lake. This could be ugly –
             as the bishop said at the door of the witch's chamber –
             and Lancelot's gone high and Mordred midward
             and bang they're in, knock-knock, and Mordred's gone
             and he's lost his head for keeps, it's literally
             bouncing, like some bowling-ball of Satan,
             into the Royal Box!

BORS: Sir Lancelot
             is Champion of the Morning. I can confirm
             we have a decapitation.

LUCAN: Aye-aye, look,
             Lancelot's in trouble too, it's his hand,
             he's took a knock.

BORS: Looks like a fingernail.

LUCAN: Devoted ladies, I know you'll be shocked to hear
             the news on that fingernail, we'll keep you posted.
             We're Lucan for Love.

BORS: And Bors for England.

WATERCUP: I've cracked it!

WATERCUP takes the Almanack to LILY, as GAWAIN departs the tent, healed.

WATERCUP: You drink this red elixir, and it makes
             Time go faster…so you can see the future…
             you can *see the future*! Why would you want to do that.
             Why? Because you'll know what's going to happen!
             Why would you want to know that. Why, because –
             you'll have the power to change it! Why would you want
             to have that. Look – I don't know – it's, it's a potion!
             And this blue elixir makes Time…stand still,
             like an antidote…I could use this, I could use this…

31

to make the lady love me! If she loved me
I would make the world a better place! To work…
Rose-petals, sage, carnation, for the red…
Lilac, hydrangea, bindweed, for the blue…

MORDRED comes, carrying his head.

WATERCUP: Decapitation. That'll be half a crown.
MORDRED: Are you trying to be funny?

LANCELOT comes, holding his finger gingerly, taking out his silver wallet.

LANCELOT: Woodland people ahoy!
Damn little bit peeled off here, not very clever.
A crown for your pains, now cure me, little mice.

WATERCUP takes the payment; LILY looks at his finger and signs a diagnosis.

WATERCUP: <u>Fingernail.</u> And <u>Toffee-nose.</u>
LANCELOT: What you say there?
WATERCUP: Nothing, sir. (Lily, it's him, my rival.
I ought to challenge him, man-to-man! I know,
I know I <u>have to be true to my healer's oath…</u>)

LANCELOT goes into the tent. WATERCUP shows LILY a page from the Almanack.

WATERCUP: Lily, see these plants? Go to the forest,
gather them all…take two different baskets,
mark one red and mark one blue. – Now, sir…

WATERCUP goes into the tent. LILY signs to MORDRED to wait. She goes into the tent and returns with a fold-out chair and a copy of HAIL! magazine. MORDRED sits, his HEAD reading the magazine. LILY goes back into the healing tent, comes out with two baskets. ELAINE comes by, with her commonplace book.

ELAINE: Ah, simple girl, off on some country errand.

LILY just looks at her. Then she heads into the woods.

ELAINE: Oh. You are Sir Mordred, the Black Knight.
You did very well.

MORDRED: I would have won on points
but that's not how they judge it, is it.

ELAINE: No…

MORDRED: It's so unfair. I *had* him.

ELAINE: Tell me, Black Knight,
do you know where they cure the serious injuries?

MORDRED gives her a look, as his BODY points at the healing tent.

ELAINE: That *waterboy* is healing Lancelot?
My knight is in the hands of *Watercup*?

MORDRED: Only cos he's rich. If you're like me
you have to wait your turn.

ELAINE: I'm not like you.
I'm the Lady of The Woods, but history
will sing my name in unison with that
of Lancelot.

MORDRED: Not according to these pictures.
Look, he's always standing by the Queen.
The two of them together. Then the King,
then behind them, look, there's all these little people.

ELAINE: That's…perspective, Mordred.
The people are far away, so they look small.

MORDRED: They sent them far away? Because they were small?

ELAINE: Er, no, it's not important –

MORDRED: They're not important?
Why, because they're small?

ELAINE: Please be quiet.

WATERCUP emerges.

WATERCUP: Elaine! You've come to watch me at my work?

ELAINE: You wish. I've come to see if my Champion
has had his fingernail restored to health.

WATERCUP: I did my best.

ELAINE: Yes well that's your job.
Now excuse me, I'm in love and you're in the way.

ELAINE goes into the tent. WATERCUP sighs.

WATERCUP: Sir Mordred, I will see you
for free this time and every time. I believe
good health should be a public service.

MORDRED: Do you.
And the small people out there, I don't suppose
that applies to the small people.

WATERCUP: What small people.

MORDRED: They were sent away, you can't see them.

WATERCUP: Ri-ight... In return,
will you help me test a couple of new products
and ask no questions of me?

MORDRED: I'm your man.

WATERCUP: It's really just a red drink and a blue drink.

LANCELOT and ELAINE emerge from the tent. LILY comes from the woods with her baskets full, and goes in, followed by WATERCUP and MORDRED.

ELAINE: What do you think of the poem, Sir Lancelot?

LANCELOT: Oh? Tremendous. Love the way it rhymes
here and there, and then, doesn't. Cracking stuff.

ELAINE: It's about a gallant knight, it's a poem of love
for the bravest knight in the world!

LANCELOT: That's tremendous.

ELAINE: It's about how a lady loves him, and one day,
at a Tournament, across a crowded greensward,
he notices this lady and their eyes meet,
and he falls in love with her.

LANCELOT: Oh that's cracking stuff.
I like a good yarn!

ELAINE: No it's based on real life.

LANCELOT: Is it, now. Real life, eh. Dum-de-dum...
Don't reckon I've met the blighter.
Is he one of the Lancashire Dum-de-dums? Well now,
I wouldn't say no to a crack at him.

ELAINE: It's you!
        You are Sir Dum-de-dum! The verse was written
        by the lady who's in love with you, and the girl
        you fall in love with wrote the lines, and *I* –
        am the writer of the poem!

LANCELOT: Slow down there,
        that's three whole different ladies.

ELAINE: No it's not!
        Take out Sir Dum-de-dum and in its place
        say Lancelot!

LANCELOT: You want me to take the place
        of Dum-de-dum? He won't take that lying down.

ELAINE: There *is* no Dum-de-dum!

LANCELOT: So he died in battle?
        Saves me the trouble, eh!

GUINEVERE comes by and sees ELAINE.

GUIN: Oh look, a fan club.
        Is the Queen allowed to join?

LANCELOT: Look here, Guin, it's a poem
        this little lady's done. It's about
        real life. There's these three gorgeous fillies
        all vying for this fellow Dum-de-dum,
        but then he's slain in combat, and all Lancashire's
        in mourning. Damn, I gave away the ending.

GUINEVERE snatches the poem.

GUIN: *The woods are wide, Sir Dum-de-dum*
        The path is only narrow,
        Still I abide, Sir Dum-de-dum
        My heart pierced by Love's arrow…
        It's crap. I need a drink. Where'd you find this?

(Sees ELAINE.)   Oh, hello, is it yours? It's very good.
        But I never heard of this Dum-de-dum.

LANCELOT: Passed away,
rest his soul. Bit of a star.

ELAINE: No – no –
it's just a space for any knight whose name
is in three parts.

LANCELOT: Tremendous.

GUIN: You mean syllables?

LANCELOT: Hang on, well, *Lance*, that's one. *Lance-a*, that's two…er…
this poetry lark is pretty technical, no?

GUIN: *The woods are big, Sir* – Hobbyhorse
And I am only small,
But yet I love, Sir – Marmalade
As long as the leaves fall.
The sky is blue, Sir – Bellyflop**,** this is fun!

LANCELOT: You show grave disrespect to the memory
of brave Sir Dum-de-dum, my dear.

GUIN: Do I really.

LANCELOT: You do.

GUIN: I do.

LANCELOT: You do.

GUIN: I do, do I?
Do you?

LANCELOT: I do.

GUIN: I do.

LANCELOT: I do.

ELAINE: Excuse me,
your Majesty, um, can I have my poem back?

GUINEVERE gives the poem back to LANCELOT.

GUIN: There, my love, you can blow your nose in springtime.

LANCELOT gives it back to ELAINE and wraps her hand round it.

LANCELOT: You keep that safe, little lady,
in memory of Sir Dum-de-dum, a good man
who fell in the field, the pride of Lancashire.

GUINEVERE and LANCELOT go. ELAINE follows. MORDRED emerges from the tent, fully recovered, with a bottle of Red Elixir. WATERCUP and LILY follow, WATERCUP still studying the pictures, LILY carrying a bottle of the Blue Elixir.

WATERCUP: Now, this red one makes Time fly…
and the blue one makes Time stand still… Oh Lily,
the power to alter Time…
What are you asking me? <u>Will I use that power</u>
<u>responsibly…or like a complete</u> – Lily,
that's just not acceptable signage.
I will use my power for Love, as a Knight should do!

MORDRED: So I drink this?

WATERCUP: Just a sip, just to try it…

MORDRED drinks the Red Elixir. Strange trill of music.

WATERCUP: What do you feel?

MORDRED: Nothing.

LILY: Wast o amser! [12]

MORDRED: Nothing at all but…*rage*, murderous rage!
That the House of Uther and this upstart villain Arthur
should sit on the throne while I, the spawn of Evil,
slouch in the gutters! But I shall bide my time,
bear the blows, endure the humiliation,
for the day will come when I will rise to power,
and the Small People will rise, and in their name
I shall put this Realm to the sword. Blood shall foam
in every forest, corpses shall be strewn
like mown grass on each village green, for I
am Mordred, nemesis of Camelot,
nightmare of all England!

WATERCUP: Don't…drink any more just yet.
– Lily, the antidote –

[12]   Waste of time!

LILY passes WATERCUP the Blue Elixir.

WATERCUP: All that evil
has probably made you thirsty, try this.
MORDRED: Is it the souls of my enemies?
WATERCUP: Er…yes.

MORDRED drinks the Blue Elixir, a strange opposing trill.

MORDRED: I mean to – I mean I need to – I need to…
I need to do some work on my jousting.
Then I'll be the best…well…better, can't win 'em all.
Did I tell you what happened at Lincoln?
I fell from my horse. But so did my opponent.

WATERCUP takes the Blue Elixir away and MORDRED walks away.

WATERCUP: It works, he flew to the future – then he came back!
That must be Mordred's destiny, he'll become
the Enemy of the Realm, did you hear him ranting?
The red one makes Time fly!
The blue one makes Time slow down to nothing…
Elaine believes she's destined to be loved
by Lancelot… and, if she drank the red,
then that would come true… but what if she drinks the blue?
She'll be…<u>stupid for eternity</u> she's not stupid!
I could keep her here in the present, in the moment,
never moving towards her destiny, and I –
would have eternity to change her mind!
And when she does, and falls in love with me,
I shall be the very flower of chivalry –
Sir Watercup! And if anything goes wrong,
we'll use the red as an antidote…To the forest!

*WATERCUP goes into the forest. LILY puts her head in her hands, then follows.
Music. The HERALD, with ARTHUR, GUINEVERE and all the KNIGHTS.*

HERALD: King Arthur and Queen Guinevere of England!
It is decreed that Sir Lancelot of the Lake
is Champion of the Morning!
Please show your appreciation of the great
Knights of Castle Camelot, past and present!

LANCELOT, GAWAIN, MORDRED, LUCAN and BORS take applause.

HERALD: In celebration of our national sport,
and recognition of the love and justice
by which he reigns in England, King Arthur
and his Queen will distribute alms to his poorer subjects.

ARTHUR and GUINEVERE distribute food to the audience. The HERALD sings.

HERALD: *What will be*
What will be
Clambering into the apple tree
Gazing down at the glittering town
A nobody
What will be

What's to come
What's to come
On the horizon beating a drum
Looking for love or what it's made of
Dum-de-dum
What's to come
What happens now
What happens now
Another deep breath another deep bow
Fight or fly, the light goes by
Any old how
What happens now

What has been
What has been
The sights I've seen and haven't seen
Are the same again the moment when
I leave the scene
What has been

What will be
What will be
Clambering into the apple tree
Gazing down at the glittering town
A nobody
What will be

ARTHUR: Love, time, and a picnic, what do you say,
try beating that! Good luck! That's the big three,
love, a picnic and yes, what the other one was.

GUIN: Time.

ARTHUR: Waits for no, what, no parsnips, eh?
no flies on them, Time flies, it was only this morning
it feels I was just a nipper –

GUIN: Oh here we go.

ARTHUR: A boy in the woods, the trees, nothing like trees,
try beating trees, you can't! You learn your trade,
king in my case, but in *your* case, well, perhaps,
a humble, sort of, craft-type thing...and in *your* case?
Beggar maybe, with not a care in the world...
Then there's the dreamer there, look, miles away
in the parish of young love...send my regards,
won't you, I used to tend a plot there! Now,
let me guess, I'm good at this...oh, a housewife,
cooking and darning, seeing to all his needs!
Now *you* look thick! I mean thick as thieves, like friends!
and that's a trade of a kind, ask me no questions,
tell me no lies, and so we pass our days,

days and nights and hot and cold and soon
we're older now and young at heart are we not,
old as the woman we feel, so we're young, eh! Dearest...
What next, I forget, you forget, we forget together,
a carnival of forgetting! clouds go by,
and the firelight to come, what do you say!
One day today will be your, your, your heyday.
But you won't know till it's gone and that's a promise!
For all the world is a – what, it's all something, eh,
it's where, where stuff goes on, eh? Oh I *had* it –
can't for the life of me *think* what all the world is!

GUIN: Thank God for that, we can eat.

LANCELOT: That's cracking stuff,
Your Majesty.

Applause. THE KNIGHTS start drinking. LANCELOT spreads a blanket for the Royal picnic. WATERCUP and LILY creep back, each with a basket of plants.

WATERCUP: I don't *care* what you think, I am in love,
I don't care what *I* think! I have the power
to alter Time, and, in the name of love
I shall serve my Lady Elaine the Blue Elixir
and preserve her beauty for eternity
in my company.

LILY: O ti'n yfarch o bidin. [13]

WATERCUP: I don't even know that sign. I am in love,
sister, there is nothing to be done
but everything!

WATERCUP and LILY go into the tent.

ARTHUR: Lancelot, Champion, join us!

LANCELOT: I thought perhaps Your Majesties might like
a little time?

[13]   Oh you're such a penis.

GUIN: We had our time already.
                       Sit down, chief.
ARTHUR: The Champion's always welcome
                       at my table, or my blanket, eh?
GUIN: Especially
                       welcome in your blanket.
ARTHUR: That's right,
                       especially at a picnic! But look here,
                       it's a square blanket, now there's one whole side
                       where no one sits! Is there not a guest to join us?

ELAINE appears, with her own little picnic things. They see her.

LANCELOT: Now you mention it –
GUIN: No there's no one. Three for lunch.
LANCELOT: Well look, I can fix it, there: the Round Blanket!

LANCELOT fashions the blanket into a circle. ELAINE sets up her own picnic.

ARTHUR: I say, that's a corking move, now it doesn't feel
          like anybody's missing!
GUIN: Nobody's missing.
ARTHUR: The Round Blanket. Not just a Champion
          but also a bit of a, what –
GUIN: A dab-hand. Husband,
          in recognition of his glorious triumph
          I shall weave a tapestry of him, for which purpose
          it is essential that I study him
          closely and at length.
ARTHUR: Indeed, my dear!
          You really are a craftsman! I should say
          crafts-*woman* (yes why not) a woman of craft
          indeed. You craft away!
GUIN: It is essential
          also that I measure his dimensions,
          so my work is true to life.
ARTHUR: True to life, eh?

	Bravo, I love to see a master at work!
	Or a mistress I should say!
GUIN:	Shut up.
ARTHUR:	Heigh-ho!

GUINEVERE starts measuring LANCELOT's dimensions, ARTHUR eats his picnic.

LUCAN:	All right, have we got it down: Gawain goes first.
	A minute with the bird. If the bird yields, *(ELAINE.)*
	your booze is free till Christmas, if she doesn't –
	who drew second?
GAWAIN:	Damn whoever drew it,
	we shan't be needing second.
MORDRED:	I drew second.
LUCAN:	Who drew second?
MORDRED:	I did, I'm right here, lads.
LUCAN:	Was it you, Bors?
BORS:	I drew fourth.
MORDRED:	I DREW SECOND!
LUCAN:	All right, don't rust your armour. I drew third.
	Floor is yours, Big G.

GAWAIN approaches ELAINE.

GAWAIN:	May I join ye, lass, ye look very down in the mouth.
ELAINE:	It depends how long it is.
GAWAIN:	How long what is?
ELAINE:	Your name.
GAWAIN:	My name's Gawain.
ELAINE:	Not long enough.

GAWAIN goes back, LUCAN and MORDRED laugh at him.

GAWAIN:	Typical English lass, she wouldn't know
	a real man if it bit her. I was about to
	but the timing wasnae right.
LUCAN:	Who drew second?

MORDRED: I DREW SECOND!

MORDRED approaches ELAINE.

MORDRED: Lady, I am Mordred.
ELAINE: I know that. Mordred what.
MORDRED: Mordred – I don't know.
ELAINE: Go away.
MORDRED: Right.

MORDRED goes back, GAWAIN and LUCAN laugh at him.

MORDRED: Oh I'm a numbskull!
                    I forgot to tell her what happened at Lincoln.
LUCAN: Shame.
                    In the next life, sunshine. My go.

LUCAN approaches ELAINE.

LUCAN: Sweetheart, let me tell you my name, it's long,
                so I'll pour us out some wine, and by and by
                we'll make acquaintance. Now my name in full –
ELAINE: I know your name, and know you are widely known
                as Lucan of the Little Cock. I presume
                there's a cockerel on your family crest.
LUCAN: There – is,
                yes, a cockerel, not to scale, but *rampante*,
                sanguine on a field of, er…chevrons.

LUCAN goes back, deflated. GAWAIN and MORDRED laugh at him. BORS approaches ELAINE. She glares at him, he does a U-turn.

BORS: Not my type.
GAWAIN: Shoulda bitten her.
MORDRED: Not my sign.
LUCAN: No sense of humour at all, that one. Chin-chin!

The KNIGHTS booze together. WATERCUP, with a jug of the Blue Elixir, and LILY come out of the tent.

WATERCUP: This is…going to end…in tears. You're right for once!

	Tears of happiness! When she drinks this drink
	she'll stay here in the moment forever,
	and everything I ever meant to tell her
	I'll come to in my *own time!* My lady,
	would you care for a glass of wine?
ELAINE:	I would not. I am having a pie.
WATERCUP:	This would go well
	with pie.
ELAINE:	Your wine is blue, fool. I would never
	drink blue wine.
WATERCUP:	They, brew it in the Chapel,
	the, er, the monks.
ELAINE:	I am a Christian.
	It's my Christian duty to drink what is made by monks.
WATERCUP:	That's very well put, my lady.

ELAINE drinks a deep draught of the Blue Elixir.

WATERCUP:	Lady Elaine? Lady Elaine?
	It's working, I can feel it. Now's my time…
	Lady Elaine, O Lady of The Woods,
	I have loved you since that moment in the forest
	when first I did set eyes upon you. Yea,
	I am rude and humbly born, and yet my heart
	is pure, my soul is true, my troth is plighted.
ELAINE:	Dum.
WATERCUP:	What did you say?
ELAINE:	De dum.
WATERCUP:	Lady Elaine?
ELAINE:	Dum…de dum…I love…
WATERCUP:	Yes? Yes?
ELAINE:	I love…this piece of pie.
WATERCUP:	You love – the piece of pie?
ELAINE:	It is a pie.
	Some of a pie. I love it.
WATERCUP:	Good, that's good,

I like pie, too, we could talk pie,

couldn't we, have a chat about favourite pies.

ELAINE: I want *this* pie. It is all brown.

WATERCUP: Elaine,

don't look at the pie, look at me.

ELAINE: I love…

WATERCUP: You love – ?

ELAINE: I love the crust of the pie.

WATERCUP: Yes, moving on –

ELAINE: I love the crust of…the crust. Oh. Oh yes.

A ladybird. It is every…thing…I want…

from…a ladybird. Red parts. Black parts.

WATERCUP: Lily! What have I done?

LILY comes out.

WATERCUP: My love has become quite boring! <u>What do you mean
'become' quite boring</u> – look, she can't even see me!

LILY waves her hand in front of ELAINE's eyes.

ELAINE: Hello fingers… Farewell fingers…

Hello fingers… Farewell fingers…

WATERCUP: Oh God!

The red, the red, we have to make the red!

WATERCUP and LILY rush back into their tent

ARTHUR: My Guinevere, my Queen,

the day draws on, daylight, daylong, my dearest,

shall we steal unto our bower?

GUIN: Talk in English.

You're king of where they have to. Yes, let's do it.

Sir Lancelot has become a lover of poems.

He can pun on himself in private.

GUINEVERE stalks off with ARTHUR. LANCELOT approaches ELAINE.

LANCELOT: Guess what, finished my homework, done my counting:

	Lance-a-lot, three syllables, may I sit?
	I'm all yours for a jiffy! How about that?
	Lady? Lady Poet?
ELAINE:	Look a white thread.
	Then a gold thread. Then a blue thread. Then a white thread.
LANCELOT:	Embroidery your thing, eh? Cracking stuff.
ELAINE:	I love the white thread. Look. An ant.
LANCELOT:	Oh yes.
	There he goes, little feller. Marvellous. Yes…
	All that aside, I expect you'd like to know
	what it's like to be a Champion!
ELAINE:	Hello
	speck of dust. Farewell speck of dust.
LANCELOT:	Hmm. Yes. *(To the KNIGHTS.)* You boys got any wine left?
LUCAN:	We're missing you, lad, get *in* here!
GAWAIN:	If ye can spare
	a moment for your friends, ye great big nancy!

LANCELOT abandons ELAINE for the livelier KNIGHTS. WATERCUP and LILY come out of the healing tent with jugs of the Red Elixir.

WATERCUP:	Keep those there in case we need them… Lady Elaine,
	how are you feeling?
ELAINE:	Feeling…
	Feeling. Fee Ling. Feeeeeeeeeeeeeeeee…

LANCELOT raises an empty bottle

LANCELOT:	Charming, *that* is! Wait for the Champion, won't you?
LUCAN:	The case, Bors!
BORS:	We finished the case, it's empty.
	I suggested moderation, but –
LUCAN:	Shut it, four-eyes.
	We're out of booze!
LANCELOT:	Ridiculous!
GAWAIN:	Yer lightweights,
	ye didnae bring enough!

MORDRED: Look over there!

LANCELOT: That water-chap, he's got a whole bloody cellar!
              Well spotted, Bors.

MORDRED: Actually it was me.

LUCAN: Four-eyes, you saved the day!

MORDRED: If I could just mention –

GAWAIN: Boys, it's a Castle-Crawl!

KNIGHTS: CASTLE-CRAWL!

The KNIGHTS descend upon WATERCUP's supply of Red Elixir.

WATERCUP: Excuse me, it's/not wine –

LANCELOT: /Good day Sir Beaujolais…
              How now Sir Côtes du Rhône…

WATERCUP: I say it's not wine,
              it's medicine!

LUCAN: Then it's going to make me better,
              water-monkey!

*LUCAN pushes WATERCUP over. The KNIGHTS start guzzling the Red Elixir.
ARTHUR and GUINEVERE return from the bower.*

ARTHUR: Oh look, high jinks! Try beating that!

GUIN: They're drunk.
              They're a disgrace.

ARTHUR: They are the soul of England,
              the noblest knights of the Kingdom!

*The KNIGHTS have all stopped drinking. They feel strange. The Red Elixir
takes effect. LANCELOT runs to GUINEVERE.*

LANCELOT: Guinevere, you are mine, I can wait no longer!

He kisses her passionately.

ARTHUR: I say, love in abundance, eh, good friends,
              good chums, eh, soul mates, what?

LUCAN runs to LANCELOT's side, and BORS to ARTHUR's.

LUCAN: I am Lucan for Love!
                I will live and die for a Lady! (When I get one.)
BORS: I will live and die for my King, I am Bors for England!
ARTHUR: Well thank you, Bors, but let's not take sides.

GAWAIN squares up to LANCELOT.

GAWAIN: Let's not take sides, ye say? *Let's not take sides?*
                This ladies' man is threatening the union
                of honourable knights!
LANCELOT: Name your weapon,
                ragamuffin.

MORDRED attempts to take centre stage.

MORDRED: It is I, Sir Mordred,
                whom am your Foe. I am the son of –
GUIN: Crikey,
                I'm having what they're having.

The KNIGHTS freeze in tense stand-off, as GUINEVERE swigs one of the bottles.

GUIN: Stuff England and stuff Camelot, I want you!

GUINEVERE leaps on LANCELOT and they fall to the ground, writhing.

ARTHUR: Shall we take five, perhaps, I think things are getting
            a little Mediterranean here…
MORDRED: It is I,
                Sir Mordred, who –
GAWAIN: For real men everywhere!

GAWAIN hauls LANCELOT up and thumps him. All the KNIGHTS draw daggers.

LUCAN: Lucan for Love!

LUCAN kills GAWAIN.

BORS: Bors for England!

BORS kills LUCAN.

LANCELOT: Lancelot
for Guinevere and for pleasure.

LANCELOT kills BORS, then suddenly kneels before ARTHUR.

LANCELOT: The fellowship is broken. I am to blame,
my lord, my liege, my friend. I yield to you
your Guinevere, and vow to live a life
consecrated to God.

ARTHUR: I see, yes well,
all's well that ends, well, not so terribly well,
but, boys will be boys eh, swings and roundabouts.

GUINEVERE kneels too.

GUIN: My shame is overwhelming. I too
shall live a life of penitence, but not,
I ought to point out, in the same place *he* does. *(LANCELOT.)*

ARTHUR: What a sad end to the story.

MORDRED stabs ARTHUR in the back.

MORDRED: Call that sad?
Notice me *now*, do you?

ARTHUR: I say, I'm dying,
killed by an unknown hand.

MORDRED: It was me, it was me!
King Mordred!

LANCELOT: Not any more.

LANCELOT kills MORDRED from a kneeling position. ARTHUR dying.

LANCELOT: Still got it.

ARTHUR: Thus I die, and thus all England
perishes with me...

*He dies. LANCELOT and GUINEVERE praying. ELAINE catatonic, the rest dead.
LILY and WATERCUP creep back. LILY signs to WATERCUP.*

WATERCUP: <u>That went well</u>.
Oh, what have we done? All right, <u>what have *I* done</u>.

LILY: Edrycha ar y llun! [14]

WATERCUP: Oh sure, look at the picture,
a drop of the blue – they're dead, Lily, they're dead!
They drank the red and went into the future
where they *died* – cos that's what happens in the future!
Lancelot's still alive, look, he's praying,
when he opens his eyes he'll kill us! Oh Lily,
I wanted to be a Knight and have a lady,
but I destroyed all England! I'm going to be hanged!
What? Nothing, that's pretty much it. Oh God!
Concentrate, concentrate, yes, the red and the blue,
one counteracts the other, but we're past that,
what's next, I didn't see that…it's a violet drink,
we mix the two…we drink the violet drink,
and…an old man in a pointy hat will come…
and all will be well, the old man in the pointy hat
will save us! Quick, let's mix the two together…

They mix the last dregs of Red and Blue. WATERCUP drinks. LILY isn't so sure.

WATERCUP: What are you waiting for? My only friend,
I don't – want to be alone with whatever happens.

LILY sighs and also drinks the Violet Elixir.

WATERCUP: We are going to be all right, Lily, I feel it.
I hear something, he's coming, it must be him,
the old man in the pointy hat! We're saved!

MRS GORMAN, the toilet cleaner, wheels on her trolley and stops it outside the Conveniences. She goes in and out, cleaning, and hangs a timetable outside.

WATERCUP: What are you doing. Excuse me, what are you doing?

MRS G.:   Doin' me job.

[14]   Look at the picture!

WATERCUP: But you – do you know a man
              who's old, with a pointy hat?
MRS G.:   What's it to you, love.
WATERCUP: I, um, murdered the, well, I accidentally murdered
              just about everyone here, and I believe
              a man in a pointy hat will come from nowhere
              and put it all right!
MRS G.:   You do?
              Not a churchgoer myself, but: free country.
WATERCUP: It isn't a country at all!
              I ruined it! Can't you do that another time?
MRS G.:   This is the time I do it.
WATERCUP: What's that sign?
MRS G.:   It tells me I were here.
              I tick the box to show all's fine and dandy.
WATERCUP: Fine and dandy? Fine and dandy? The king
              lies dead and it's fine and dandy?
MRS G.:   I'm done now, pet.
              I do my job and you do yours. Goodbye.

MRS GORMAN wheels her trolley away. WATERCUP sinks in despair.

WATERCUP: A toilet cleaner? A toilet cleaner! I want
              my old man with a pointy hat and I get
              a toilet cleaner! Oh God…

He dissolves. LILY looks on with scorn, fills a cup of water, throws it over him.

WATERCUP: Plan B. We'll run away. Let's go. Let's go!
LILY: Ni angen clirio'r llanast ma! [15]
WATERCUP: Clear up the mess?
              That was Plan A. Plan B is running like hell.
              Lily, Lily, please!

---

[15]   We need to clear up this mess!

LILY won't budge. WATERCUP flees into the forest. LILY sighs and waves goodbye. Enter MERLIN, an old man with a pointy hat. He advances on LILY.

MERLIN: Good God…What happened here?
I got here fast as I could – but I'm too late!
Arthur slain, and all his knights, oh Heavens!
The Queen – Lancelot – gone from the earthly sphere!
Catastrophe, oh! Girl, what happened here?
Girl – do you not speak?
Show me! What happened here? <u>There was a lady,</u>
yes, <u>pushing a trolley,</u> what happened next?
<u>She…cleaned the toilets…then she went away</u>.

MERLIN looks like thunder. He points at the bodies.

MERLIN: I mean – WHAT HAPPENED HERE!

LILY pretends not to have noticed the bodies. She pretends to be startled, then shrugs.

MERLIN: Evidently an imbecile. What's this then…

He finds a red-stained bottle, tastes the dregs.

MERLIN: *Tempus Fugit.* In a crude form, very crude.
Some careless spell's been cast. I can restore them,
but a journey lies before them, through the Valley
of Foul Despair, through fires of – oh I say.
(He sees ELAINE.) A flibbertigibbet? A will-o'-the-wisp? A beauty…
Young lady, can you tell me your name?

ELAINE: Pie. No pie.

MERLIN sees her blue-stained goblet, tastes the dregs.

MERLIN: *Tempus Obstinat.*
But like a fool would make it. She needs *that* stuff,
    (The Red Elixir.)
but it has to be brewed properly. Come with me,
we'll pick some forest flowers and pass the time

in idle chatter, and the somewhat many years
between us we shall shorten to a moment…

LILY points at the bodies and signs to MERLIN.

MERLIN: What's that? <u>What about them?</u>
        <u>You're old…you have a pointy hat…help them</u>.
        I'm helping this lady first.

LILY: Helpa nhw gynta! [16]

MERLIN: They need more than an antidote. They need
        to seek the Chapel Perilous. The way
        is bleak, the journey long. Hard by a river,
        in the ruins left by Roman infidels,
        there shines a light, a green light, a – what?

LILY is pointing to the green light on the top of the Chapel. MERLIN ignores her.

MERLIN: Not now, I am making a speech. Hard by a river,
        in the ruins left – will you stop that?
        In a wilderness to the north and west, there shines
        a light so green – look I have a pointy hat
        and I'm speaking!

LILY: Hen ffwl, ma fe reit na! [17]

MERLIN turns and sees the Chapel.

MERLIN: Well. Yes. *That* Chapel Perilous. I knew that.
        Right. To work.
        Barley, fainites, crosses, kings…

He waves his wand. The BODIES stand, raise their arms, cross their fingers, and troop out to the Chapel, as if entranced.

THE BODIES: *Barley, fainites, crosses, kings*
              Truce, barsies, screwsies, scrims
              Pax, skinges, creases, creams
              Barley, fainites, crosses, kings

[16]   Help them first!

[17]   You old fool, it's right there!

MERLIN: Satisfied?

MERLIN points to his hat, then leads ELAINE into the forest. A distant howling. WATERCUP appears elsewhere, glancing desperately behind him.

WATERCUP: Oh Elaine, what have I done?
I abandoned you, I deserted my dear sister,
I murdered Knights, I slew the King of England,
and something in this wood is trying to kill me!

Exit, pursued by a fearsome WHITE KNIGHT in full armour, waving its sword and howling. It runs away into the trees. Silence. LILY is left alone.

LILY: Bwyta. Yfed. Ugain mined. Cewch bant. [18]

END OF ACT ONE

---

[18]   Eat. Drink. Twenty minutes. Go away.

ACT TWO

HERALD: *Here's what you missed*
If you were being kissed
Or doing your Christmas list
Or losing money hand-over-fist
Or maybe you were just getting pist-
Achios from the pistachio-tree
But if so, you better listen to me…
Watercup is in love with Elaine,
Elaine thinks he's a twit
So he learned to make Time fast and slow
But he made a pig's ear of it
So he ran away and there's hell to pay
And now there's a mystical man
With a towering hat – if you got all that
You're a better man than I *am*

MERLIN is interrogating LILY. ELAINE, restored, looks on.

MERLIN: Let's go over it again. You say your brother
brewed the potions. <u>Yes</u>. From a book? <u>Yes</u>.
So where is this mysterious book? <u>Right there</u>.
Why didn't you just say that the first time?
<u>Nobody was…watching</u>. What does she mean
nobody was watching?

ELAINE: Her name's Lily,
she speaks some cuckoo language. She is a simple
country thing, I wish I was just like her,
I mean, I'd still talk normally, I wouldn't
live in the woods like that or wear those clothes,
but otherwise just like her.

MERLIN: I would wish you
exactly as you are…

ELAINE: Please don't wish me
anything, I've heard about your kind.
You and your big stick there.   *(Wand.)*

MERLIN: I'm sorry? Oh yes.

MERLIN looks in the Almanack. LUCAN and BORS return to the puppet tent.

LUCAN: What are you on about, Sir Bors?

BORS: I always
think it's interesting to report my dreams
to other people. That way other people
get an insight into my personality.

LUCAN: I had a dream myself, we were all fighting,
us knights, next thing I knew it were all green
and I were in some church...that's how I knew
I were dreaming, I were in church.

BORS: In *my* dream –

LUCAN: We're back,
we're live and we're Lucan for love!

BORS: And Bors for England.
This Afternoon the Passage-of-Arms will feature
local knights testing themselves in combat
against the cream of Camelot and that cream
will come out fighting.

LUCAN: It is top-level cream
and we're lapping it up at the Chapel of Sir Groevanor.

MERLIN: *Tempus Fugit, Tempus Obstinat...*
Mix them together and what...

LILY: Ma na hen ddyn mewn het bigog
yn dod a bydd popeth yn iawn! [19]

MERLIN: What's that,
me? this is not me, this is – this is –
oh no. Oh no! Nightmare!

---

[19]   An old man in a pointy hat comes, and all will be well!

ELAINE: Do you mean nightmare
in a negative way?

MERLIN: *(To LILY.)* Did he mix the two together?
<u>Yes…it was violet.</u> Did he drink the mixture?

LILY: Yeah a fi. [20]

MERLIN: A Violet Elixir, no!
This picture here, this man with a hat, this means
a figure of the future, this means
himself in the time-to-come – he has both frozen
himself in youth and conjured himself in age!
There is *Another* of him in this same forest!

ELAINE: You mean, another Watercup? That's a good thing,
isn't it, or it would be if I liked him,
but I don't so it's terrible news! Oh no!

MERLIN: And if
the two should meet, the two come face-to-face…

ELAINE: Well they'd have a lot in common.

MERLIN: Oh, poor maiden,
God save our souls. Observe the final picture:
the sundial has no dial,
the clock no hands. Time will stop forever.

ELAINE: That's bad, isn't it.

MERLIN: I have to think, *think*!

ELAINE: I think she's saying she also drank the drink.   *(LILY.)*

While MERLIN says the following, MRS GORMAN wheels her trolley on, checks the Conveniences, ticks the grid again and wheels her trolley off. No one notices.

MERLIN: What? That doesn't matter. In old age
she'd simply be some other forgotten creature,
some poor neglected dogsbody in shadow,
it's what *men* do that matters. Forest elf,
what did your brother want to be in the future?

[20]   Yes, so did I.

LILY makes the sign of riding and sound of galloping.

ELAINE: A horse!

MERLIN: A knight! He wanted to be a knight…

ELAINE: That sounded more like a horse, Lily.

LUCAN: Hey, Bors,

you ever seen *him* before?

LUCAN and BORS are looking out at the Lists.

BORS: Well it's not Sir Capenhurst, he's vert-and-argent

on a lozenge, and it's not Sir Balderton,

he's gules-and-sable horizontal, it's not

Sir Cotton Edmunds, he's /usually –

LUCAN: SHUT UP!

I don't want to know who it's not.

I want to know who it is. He's a big lad,

and he seems to be challenging anyone to fight him.

MERLIN: What did you say?

LUCAN: Take a look for yourself, old man.

He just sits there and waits, clad all in white.

They're calling him the Knight With No Name.

MERLIN looks out at the Lists, beckons LILY to join him. ELAINE comes too.

MERLIN: Forest elf, come hither. Is that your brother?

He's in…full armour…how the…hell…would *I* know.

ELAINE: It *could* be Watercup, if he were massive

and owned a horse, and we were in the future,

but he isn't, and he doesn't, and we aren't,

are we? I mean, not yet. I suppose we will be.

MERLIN: *(To BORS.)* And you've never seen that knight until this

moment?

BORS: His current average is nought over nought-

point-nought for nought.

MERLIN: What?

LUCAN: No, we've not seen him.

It's like he dropped from the sky. The local knights

have melted away, they don't fancy the challenge. Ladies
are swooning, standing up again, seeing the stranger
and swooning again!

BORS: The Crusaders of St John's
Ambulance Service have got their work cut out.

LUCAN: Here comes Mordred, *he's* up for the challenge...

MERLIN, LILY and ELAINE leave the puppet tent.

MERLIN: Tell me about her brother, what does he look like?

ELAINE: A nobody. When I first saw him, I said
oh look, there's a nobody there, and –

MERLIN: What's *she* saying?

LILY is signing furiously to MERLIN.

MERLIN: He...loves...the stupid lady. He loves you?

ELAINE: Are you calling me stupid?

MERLIN: Time could stop forever!
This is not a time to take things personally!

ELAINE: I might be stupid sometimes, but at least
I don't look a hundred and ten.

MERLIN: That's quite absurd.
The consensus is I look middle-aged.

LILY: Ffwls.
Ma brawd fi'n mynd i dod nol achos
ma fe mewn cariad a fi'n
gwybod be ma fe fel. [21]

MERLIN: You say he'll come back here?

ELAINE: He can do as he likes, it won't mean a thing to me.

MERLIN: Won't mean a thing? Except that Time will cease!
The White Knight *cannot* meet him!

[21] Fools.
My brother will come back because
he's in love, and
I know what he's like.

ELAINE:	Explain again,
	what has the Knight to do with Watercup?
MERLIN:	The Knight *is* Watercup!
ELAINE:	No *seriously*
	what has the Knight to do with Watercup.
MERLIN:	Oh,
	ignoramus!
ELAINE:	Don't cast a spell on me!
MERLIN:	I'm *calling* you an ignoramus.
ELAINE:	Oh.
	Phew.
MERLIN:	The Knight was Watercup in the past.
	Watercup will *be* the Knight in the future.
	Oblivion will follow if they meet.
ELAINE:	But why?
MERLIN:	What? Because they are – the same!
ELAINE:	The same as what?
MERLIN:	Each other! The same person!
ELAINE:	What's wrong with that? If I met myself-when-young
	I'd give myself advice on what to do
	when I meet myself-when-old, so when I did
	I wouldn't be afraid, I'd thank myself
	for my wise words…
MERLIN:	Enough!
ELAINE:	…I would give myself
	a set of bath oils, that's what you give old ladies.
MERLIN:	They must *never* meet!
ELAINE:	Meet as in shake hands,
	or wave across a room? Or simply pass by
	at a village fair? How do you *measure* meeting?
	And surely if he meets his future self,
	then his future self met *him* when he was young
	in his past self, but we know the world was fine
	because the youth grew old in these same woods
	and met a young lad in/ the future –

MERLIN: /It's – against the Law!

ELAINE: The law of what?

MERLIN: The Law
            of the Space-Time Continuum.

ELAINE: The what?

MERLIN: The Space-Time Continuum.

ELAINE: The what?

MERLIN: The Space-Time Continuum.

ELAINE: The what?

MERLIN: Continuum.

ELAINE: The –

MERLIN: Continuum. Quantum.

ELAINE: The what?

MERLIN: Continuum. Quantum. Quark.
            Quasar.

ELAINE: But –

MERLIN: Continuum.

ELAINE: But –

MERLIN: *(Pointing.)*   Hat.

ELAINE: But –

MERLIN: Hat.

ELAINE: I –

MERLIN: Magic.

ELAINE: I –

MERLIN: Hat.

ELAINE: Oh. I think I see. What can we do?

MERLIN: You, nothing. I? I must take steps
            to render a chance collision of the two
            theoretically impossible.

ELAINE: What does that mean?

MERLIN: I have to reduce the unstable atomic structure
            to fifty percent of itself.

ELAINE: What does that mean?

MERLIN: I have to destroy Watercup.

ELAINE: Oh no!

Destroy the Knight, not Watercup! I mean,
I *know* Watercup, I mean we're not best friends
but he means no harm.

MERLIN: Means no harm? He has placed
the Universe on the brink of cataclysm!

ELAINE: Yes, but he's probably kicking himself, I would be.

MERLIN: Continuum!

ELAINE: But –

MERLIN: Continuum!

ELAINE: But –

MERLIN: Hat!
He who stands guilty of this breach in Time
must pay the ultimate price. Watercup
must be destroyed. I shall observe the Lists,
make sure the White Knight stays there. You must watch
for Watercup. If he returns, send word
by the simple creature, then: I shall do
That Which Must Be Done.

MERLIN goes to the Tournament.

ELAINE: Lily, what can we do? Sshh…you're…trying to think.
I'll try to think as well… I like it quiet
when I'm trying to think… It's quiet here, I mean,
apart from someone talking. Oh that's me.
Sshh…that's better. – I think it's really unfair
Watercup has to be destroyed, I *hate*
that stupid Continuing!

LILY: Edrychwn ni mas amdano fe… [22]

ELAINE: We'll watch for him…

LILY: Os welwn ni fe… [23]

---

[22] We'll watch for him...

[23] If we see him...

ELAINE:	<u>If we see him</u>…
LILY:	Rhedwn ni bant dan gilydd… [24]
ELAINE:	<u>Run away</u>

<u>together</u>, yes! <u>No…*we'll* run away together</u>.
<u>You'll</u>…<u>run away together</u>. Oh. Yes.
<u>And never…be seen again</u>. Right. Good.
All right. A little bit sad, but…sensible,
in the circumstances, and nothing to do with me,
what Watercup gets up to, running away
or not running away. Better than having Time
and the Universe, like, end.
I suppose. There'd still be a Universe, just not
one where I'll see them again, him and his sister,
one where I call him a nobody or call her
a simple nobody – as if that matters at all!
No one would miss them much. Come on then, Lily,
let's watch at the forest edge. If we never find him,
we'll never see him again, and if we find him,
I'll never see him or you again. What a sad day
it turned to, when it started out so jolly.

ELAINE and LILY keep watch for WATERCUP. Elsewhere, WATERCUP climbs down out of a tree in the wood, with a bag.

WATERCUP: Did you see him? A huge white knight, I think I lost him,
he was *this* tall, he was breathing fire and his eyes –
Who am I talking to? – My wits are turning
for grief and sorrow, O Elaine, Elaine,
I turned you to a simpleton, and my sister,
poor Lily, you'll be blamed
for the death of Arthur and his gallant knights,
the annihilation of the Realm of England! Oh
why did I ever read that book? The red,
the blue, we are dead, or good as dead – and the violet?

[24]   We'll run away together...

Nothing came at all. No old man
in a pointy hat, no hat, no happy end!
How can I help Elaine or rescue Lily?
I'll be killed if I show my face! And that's why…
out of wolf-hairs, weasel-pelt and egg-yolk…
have I fashioned this impenetrable disguise.

He produces a rubbish blonde wig from his bag, and puts it on.

WATERCUP: I am not Watercup, nor he I was
before I took that name. To the river bank
I went, to muse upon this, and the water
spoke: *You are Dee, Poor Dee, the River-Girl.*
To the Chapel of Sir Groevanor!

He returns to the Tournament, as the drum-roll signals the afternoon's first Joust.

LUCAN: *Now* we'll see what he's made of, this White Giant
who's come from nowhere to lay down his challenge.
BORS: Mordred's on his horse now, it's a long shot,
it's a funny old game and they're under starter's orders…

ELAINE and LILY see WATERCUP arrive. So does LUCAN.

ELAINE: Who goes there?
LUCAN: Aye-aye, don't mind if I do.
What's your name, little lady?
BORS: Lucan, the Lists.
WATERCUP: I be – Poor Dee, Poor Dee the River-Girl.
I be lost in the forest. (Elaine seems restored –
and the knights are as they were – but I can't risk it,
I'll be burned for witchcraft, hung for poisoning.)

ELAINE: *(To LILY.)* Come with me, Poor Dee, we're on the lookout
for a boy in trouble, but, between ourselves,
I was getting bored of that, Lily can do it,
and you know what I'm in the mood for? Girl-talk!
WATERCUP: Who is this boy in trouble?

ELAINE: Oh some boy,
                      he's in trouble but I don't care, I do in a way,
                      you should always care, I care about him, well I don't,
                      but I do, in fact – and this is something I'd only
                      ever say to my best friend in the world
                      and that's you, by the way – deep down, I *quite like him.*

WATERCUP: You *do*?

ELAINE: Oh that's a secret!
                      Clap hands. Now turn around. Now jump up and down.
                      Now stand on one leg. Now make a wish. That's good.
                      The secret is safe. Anyway, he's a nobody,
                      and I'm destined to marry a Knight. Forget all about him,
                      cuz, can I call you cuz?

WATERCUP: Er, what's a cuz?

ELAINE: I don't know, but you're *my* cuz!

WATERCUP: Yes, er, cuz,
                      why is this boy in trouble?

ELAINE: Oh, it's nothing.
                      I think he's put the Universe in danger.

WATERCUP: He has?

ELAINE: I know, he's so silly! And this ancient
                      cove in a hat says Time will stop forever.

WATERCUP: *What???*

ELAINE: It's more polite to say *beg your pardon.*
                      But yes, the world will end, cuz.

WATERCUP: *Oh no!*

ELAINE: It's all very interesting.

WATERCUP: *Oh no! Oh no!*

ELAINE: You're a very good listener, cuz. You and me
          are going to be inseparable! Night and day
          we shall laze serenely in my leafy bower,
          cast off our clothes and talk of love together!

WATERCUP: *(Low.)* Er, very well.

ELAINE: You've a low voice.

WATERCUP: *(High.)*   Very well!

The trumpet sounds.

ELAINE: But the Passage-of-Arms is starting, I have a seat,
you'll have to wait for me, cuz!

WATERCUP: I shall wait right here!

ELAINE rushes out to the Tournament.

WATERCUP: – She likes me! Time will come to an end but *she likes me!*
I've caused the end of the world but *she quite likes me!*

WATERCUP drinks some wine he finds, then has to nip to the Knights' toilet.

BORS: All eyes on the mysterious White Horseman
as he starts his gallop, it's white against black, it's like some
game of chess if chess was played on horseback
with lances in a big field…

LUCAN: And bang!
Mordred's down, that's jousting, done and dusted,
wham-bam-Bedivere!

BORS: I'm Bors for England.

LUCAN: I'm Lucan for Love. The Nameless White Knight
sits tall in his white saddle.

BORS: *Where does he come from?*
Who is his Lady? What is his name? Just three
of the questions we'll be asking.

LUCAN: *We don't have*
the foggiest idea – that's just one
of the answers you'll get. In fact it's the only one.

ELAINE returns.

ELAINE: Who *is* that man? Where does he come from?
How could *he* be Watercup in the future,
past *or* present? The old man is demented.
Watercup is a weed, but the White Knight's
a wonder! Oh, his name must have three parts!
What's Lancelot compared to him? Cuz! Cuz?

WATERCUP comes out of the Knights'.

WATERCUP: I'm here, cuz, shall we start
serenely lazing, casting off clothes and so on?
Or you could cast off yours and I could advise you
maybe…

ELAINE: Yes, on what I should wear beneath,
in the silken colours of the new Knight I favour,
and I'd do the same for you.

WATERCUP: There's no *pressing* need
for you to do that, my cuz, I exist to serve you.
So where's that leafy bower you mentioned, I –
what?

ELAINE: You – just – came out of the tent for Knights.
Why?

WATERCUP: Because (good point) in my spare time, cuz,
I work with that woman who ticks the box, you see,
here's me ticking the box. Ticked it. There.

WATERCUP ticks the box.

WATERCUP: All clean back there, shipshape, no worries.

ELAINE: Oh, cuz,
we're the best friends in the world, forget all that,
all labour, duty, obligation. Our time
will be slow and soft and sensual, we shall dream
of knights together.

WATERCUP: Nights together…

ELAINE: Bold knights
and bashful knights –

WATERCUP: Oh I see what you mean, yes *knights*,
of course.

ELAINE: Of handsome knights, heroic knights,
mischievous knights and muscular knights, oho!
We shall have gay talk of knights!

WATERCUP: We certainly shall.

ELAINE: Let me tell you about the mysterious White Knight…

The HERALD bring MORDRED back, bloody. LILY assesses him.

HERALD: Water cup!

WATERCUP: Yes?

ELAINE: What do you mean, Yes?

WATERCUP: Yes, I mean – look, a water cup, right there!
That's a water cup, spot on. Table? Yes!
Picnic basket? Yes!

ELAINE: You're my funny cuz.
When you said 'water cup' it reminded me
of Watercup. How strange.

LILY is urgently showing MORDRED something from the Almanack.

MORDRED: What are you saying?
I should have dipped the lance? What do *you* know, peasant?
Heal my wounds and crawl back in your hole!

WATERCUP strides across and thumps MORDRED, laying him out.

WATERCUP: Don't talk to my sister like that!

LILY: Watercup!!!

ELAINE: *Watercup*???

LILY hugs WATERCUP. ELAINE watches in astonishment.

LILY: Mae'r dyn yn y het bigog ar dy ol di!
Rhed bant! [25]

WATERCUP: Run away? Run away?
I'm here to atone for everything, to put right
all my wrongs. Sister: heal this man.

*LILY pulls MORDRED into the healing tent. WATERCUP, heroic, turns to face
ELAINE – who thumps him.*

ELAINE: Watercup, I shall say this only once.

[25] The man in the pointy hat is after you!
Run away!

I am glad that Time will cease and the Universe
end forever, because I shall no longer
be forced to look at your ludicrous silly face.
We shall never meet again, whether the World
end right now or never.

WATERCUP: What do you mean
end? Where's the old man with the pointy hat?

ELAINE: He's at the jousts. If he finds you he will kill you!
The White Knight's *You-Grown-Up,* I mean, it's not,
that's nonsense actually, as I just watched
the Knight in action and he's not a weed like you,
Watercup, but the mad old bloke does think that,
that if you and the White Knight touch each other, all Time
will cease or something, he has a hat and he says so,
so I'm simply saying, in passing –

WATERCUP: Stop talking!

ELAINE: What? I mean *beg your pardon.*

WATERCUP: There's something I have to tell you.

ELAINE: Watercup
I've heard enough from you. What is it, though.
You can say what it is, then go away.

WATERCUP: It's about –
it's about –

ELAINE: You've no time to waste!
The old man's going to turn you into – dead!

WATERCUP: I don't care.

ELAINE: And Time will cease forever!

WATERCUP: I don't care.

ELAINE: And the Universe will end!

WATERCUP: There is something I care *more* about!

ELAINE: There is?
What?

WATERCUP: I – I – I –

LILY:	Hen ddyn!
	Het bigog! Me fe'n dod! [26]
MERLIN:	*(From off.)* Dear lady? Lady Elaine?
ELAINE:	He can't find you here!

ELAINE puts the wig back on WATERCUP, as MERLIN arrives.

ELAINE:	Look this is my cuz.
WATERCUP:	Hello I'm her cuz.
MERLIN:	Comeliness abounding…What is your name?
WATERCUP:	Poor Dee, I be, the river-girl.
MERLIN:	Pray, how
	can one man ever choose when beauty walks
	so many-petalled?
LUCAN:	And here comes Gawain,
	and ouch, there goes Gawain.
BORS:	Gawain is down,
	and the White Knight is ploughing a great white furrow
	through Camelot!
LUCAN:	There's Lancelot, he'll stop this,
	for the honour of King Arthur!
BORS:	For England!
MERLIN:	Is there any sign of the boy?
ELAINE:	No sign at all.
	Did you see a boy, Poor Dee? No, you didn't,
	did you, you're a girl.
WATERCUP:	What has this boy
	done wrong, venerable sir?
MERLIN:	He has jeopardised
	the Universe!
WATERCUP:	I'm sure he didn't mean to.
ELAINE:	I'll explain it later, cuz, it's about the Quango
	Continuing in Time and Space or something.

[26]   Old man!

        Pointy hat! He's coming!

The HERALD brings GAWAIN back, bloody and dazed.

HERALD: Watercup!

GAWAIN: Donald…where's yer trewsers…

HERALD: Watercup? WATERCUP!

WATERCUP: LILY!

LILY comes out with the healed MORDRED, brings the wounded GAWAIN in.

MERLIN: Why did she just say *Lily*?

ELAINE: It's what she calls me.

Don't you, Dee.

WATERCUP: Yes, Elaine. I mean Lily. Lily!

LUCAN: And here comes Lancelot on Boy Legend,

Lancelot of the Lake, pride of England!

BORS: He'll have to restore some pride, for this White Knight

has made a mockery of the form-book.

MERLIN: Pray

the White Knight is victorious. If he's wounded

he'll come this way and all my instincts tell me

Watercup is close by.

LUCAN: Here they come

and bang, it's over, good-night folks, and good-night

Lancelot! Amazing!

BORS: The White Knight

has vanquished every Knight of Camelot!

MERLIN: Is he riding away? Is the White Knight riding away?

LUCAN: No he's sat there on his horse. It's like he's waiting…

LILY brings the restored GAWAIN out and is showing him the Almanack.

GAWAIN: So I…wore my shield too high… Mebbe you're right.

Och I'm too old for this, I'm getting coached

by a wee lassie, I'm out.

GAWAIN joins LUCAN and BORS.

ELAINE: Cuz, Poor Dee, what did you want to tell me?

WATERCUP: Nothing, cuz, except that in the forest
I *met* a boy in trouble. He said that one day
the world would see him fight in a noble cause
against impossible odds, and for a lady.

ELAINE: Did he say who that lady was?

WATERCUP: He was about to,
when –

The HERALD comes back with the only slightly wounded LANCELOT.

HERALD: Water cup!

LANCELOT: Thanks, old bean, I can manage.
(To ELAINE.) Hey little poetry lady, I've a news-flash.
That Dum-de-dum of yours is back in business!

LILY escorts LANCELOT into the healing tent. ARTHUR and GUINEVERE arrive.

ARTHUR: Anyone seen my Knights at all? No rush,
but a giant Foe is out there on his giant, you know,
horse, and there's no one left.

GUIN: That's because your Knights
are alcoholic good-for-nothing pillocks
who haven't fought a battle since the Romans
took their toys away.

MERLIN: Arthur, hear me,
the peril is far graver than you know!

ARTHUR: Where the deuce have *you* been? You always
come when it's too late.

MERLIN: I was in the forest,
gathering my thoughts.

GUIN: Oh that's useful,
shall I make them into soup?

ARTHUR: Sir Lancelot?
Sir Gawain? Sir Mordred?

The KNIGHTS emerge. LILY is showing LANCELOT the Almanack.

LANCELOT: So you think I should take my head out of my – I say,
it's all gone quiet.

ARTHUR: Knights of Camelot,
would you mind awfully taking another crack
at the gentleman on the horse? Mordred, old chap?

MORDRED: I hereby announce my retirement from jousting,
your so-called Majesty. From this day on
I shall report on sport for the small people
who can't see over the crowd. Ninety-nine jousts.
Ninety-eight defeats. I'll always have Lincoln.

MORDRED sticks his sword in the ground and goes to the puppet tent.

ARTHUR: Gawain? Will you not challenge the White Horseman?

GAWAIN: Make way for an old dog there, the game's moved on,
I've not a clue what I'm doin', I'll be an expert.

GAWAIN sticks his sword in the ground and goes to the puppet tent.

ARTHUR: Lancelot? Champion?

LANCELOT: Well, the thing of it is,
I had a good innings, eh, perhaps this chap
is the new me, so to speak. Best of British,
Sir Dum-de-dum! Is there any prosecco going?

LANCELOT sticks his sword in the ground and goes to the puppet tent.

GUIN: *(To ARTHUR.)* Don't look at me like that. It's your gang.
Somebody pour me a double and I'll drink
to losers I have loved.

GUINEVERE joins the KNIGHTS in the puppet tent.

ARTHUR: Well. I say.
So passes the, you know,
glory that was – well, was glorious.
I don't have a speech prepared. Where's that Herald?
He could sing about, you know, sweet things ending,
make it not seem so bad. *Heigh-ho*, it could go,
in the chorus, *heigh-ho, heigh-ho, heigh-ho* oh heck.

*The WHITE KNIGHT comes, haughty, mysterious, faceless, sword raised. The
KNIGHTS cower. The WHITE KNIGHT advances on ARTHUR.*

ARTHUR: I suppose *I* have to fight him, which is, well,
not how I planned to bid ye goodbye. As I say,
I don't have a speech prepared. Perhaps you could say
my last day was my favourite day, and it was.
In fact it always was, now I think about it.
Well, here goes. For England. *Heigh-ho.*

*WATERCUP steps forth, throws off his wig, pulls Lancelot's sword from the
ground.*

WATERCUP: Sheathe your sword, your Highness, *I* shall fight him!
For the Lady of The Woods!

ELAINE: Watercup, no!

LILY: Ma hyn yn dwp, hyn yn oed i ti. [27]

MERLIN: *Watercup? No!* It cannot be!
This boy and this mysterious White Knight
are the same person, sundered by the years,
but drawn together in this place by witchcraft!
Were they to touch, then all the Universe
would crumble, and Time cease!

Everyone goes still.

MERLIN: – I am too late.
It is done. And so begins…
The Age of Oblivion.

ARTHUR: Sorry, old chap, I think we were all a bit shocked
at the crap you just came out with.

WATERCUP: Time, cease!
Universe, crumble to dust! I have no fear.
I am Watercup of the Weeds, your Majesty,
and I will fight this brute to restore the honour
of Camelot.

---

[27]   This is stupid, even for you.

MERLIN:	This cannot be!
ARTHUR:	Knights,

restrain the old boy, will you, senior moment.
Watercup of the Weeds, I salute you.
Should you triumph, I mean in theory should you triumph,
can't quite see it myself but I *am* a fan,
so in the unlikely event you be not slaughtered,
savaged, dismembered or decapitated,
what do you ask in return?

WATERCUP: What do I ask?
I ask to be admitted to the ranks
of the Legendary Knights of Camelot,
as *Sir* Watercup, so that the Lady Elaine
might find me worthy of her hand in marriage.

ELAINE: Oh! I'm going to swoon – but I'll miss something!
You like me! You quite like me!

WATERCUP: I quite love you.
'One day you shall see me fight in a noble cause
against impossible odds, and for a lady.'

ELAINE: But I thought you were a halfwit then! Now you love me
and you're going to go and die!

MERLIN: All will die!
There'll be no such thing as *anything*!

ARTHUR: Pipe down,
old boy, pipe down. *Heigh-ho* all you subjects,
young Watercup will fight. If he prevails
I shall make a Knight of him!
Let Time cease and the Universe crumble, England
loves an underdog!

*The WHITE KNIGHT and WATERCUP fight. WATERCUP falls, and the WHITE
KNIGHT stands over him, sword-point to his neck. No one can look, then suddenly.*

ELAINE runs up and kneels beneath the sword.

ELAINE: White Knight, stranger, enemy of all
            I know, please take my life – but only spare
            the life of the boy I love!

*The WHITE KNIGHT seems to ponder awhile. Then he sticks his sword in the
ground with the other swords, and extends his hand to the fallen WATERCUP.*

MERLIN: I tell you – Time will cease!

*WATERCUP and the WHITE KNIGHT clasp hands, and the KNIGHT lifts
WATERCUP to his feet. WATERCUP and ELAINE embrace.*

ARTHUR: I don't know if Time ceased or not, old man,
            but that was a corking gesture from the fellow,
            not to mention the lady. Watercup,
            for your courage in the face of quite absurd
            and faintly embarrassing odds, I do dub thee
            Sir Watercup of the Weeds. O White Knight
            who has given all of Camelot a lesson
            in arms and in good grace, will you not reveal
            your name and origins?

*The WHITE KNIGHT seems to stare at ARTHUR. Then he starts to make signs,
and WATERCUP finds he can understand them.*

WATERCUP: …I…don't know where I come from…I was walking
            in the forest, I was afraid, I cried out…
            then I saw your men on horseback…I always
            loved the jousting…when I was…a little…
            girl… I used to go to the tournaments
            and heal the fallen knights…one day my brother
            found an old book…and that day I decided
            to make myself…so big and strong…that one day
            I could fight the noblest champions of the kingdom…

*The WHITE KNIGHT notices LILY doing the same signs as she is. They move
towards each other, but MERLIN thrusts himself between them.*

MERLIN: I tell you, Time will cease! You cannot touch her!
WATERCUP: Time didn't cease when she shook me by the hand.

MERLIN:	But the White Knight isn't Watercup – she's *her!*
ARTHUR:	Then who the deuce did Watercup become?

MRS GORMAN wheels her trolley into the scene.

ELAINE:	Watercup, you became a toilet cleaner,
	and a woman, that's disappointing on every level.
MERLIN:	Do you have to do that now?
MRS G.:	Wonder of wonders,
	Merlin…
WATERCUP:	Merlin?
MRS G.:	You noticed me! 'Just some forgotten creature,
	some poor neglected dogsbody in shadow.
	For it's what *men* do that matters.'

MRS GORMAN throws off her overalls and reveals herself to be MORGANA.

MORGANA:	Do you remember, Merlin?
MERLIN:	Morgana…
	Worst nightmare! Nemesis!
ARTHUR:	Here we go again.
MERLIN:	Spawn of the Devil!
MORGANA:	Merlin, calm down, dear,
	I'm someone just like you. Except I'm slightly
	better than you at magic.
MERLIN:	That's what I mean –
	my worst nightmare! You used to look like – that!
	At the Academy –
MORGANA:	I used to look like this.
MERLIN:	But you *can't* – it was, it was centuries ago!
MORGANA:	We were partners there, in the potion-room, remember?
	You would stir your chemicals and cast your spells
	then, when the dust had settled on your usual
	wreck of smoking ruins and aberrations,
	I was left to mop things up. I did so gladly,
	Merlin, I'm doing it now.
WATERCUP:	What did you call him?

MORGANA: *(To MERLIN.)* Why are you always late? Why do you always
miss the start of the day?

MERLIN: I was – in the forest –

MORGANA: You find yourself in the forest.

MERLIN: On the path,
in sunlight, patterned sunlight…

MORGANA: Are you a child there,
a young man or an old?

MERLIN: I am – all three.
I was – thinking about the world,
how – marvellous it was, but all the while
how evil lurked behind the trees…I wished
to learn, to make the world a better place…
I thought I might find answers – in a book.

MORGANA: Was that once upon a time? Or on this day?

WATERCUP: *(To MORGANA.)* Why do you – call him Merlin? That's
my –

MERLIN: *(To WATERCUP.)* Don't touch me!

MORGANA: Oh Merlin, Merlin, Time stopped long ago.
No harm can come where we are. Take his hand.
(To MERLIN and WATERCUP.) It's your own hand, won't you take it?

MERLIN: This fool was never me.

WATERCUP: I'll never be
a fool like that!

MERLIN: I was the brightest boy
in the Academy!

MORGANA: You were the only boy.
Behind the nine bright girls.

WATERCUP: He can't be me!
I've just been made a Knight, and look at him!

MERLIN: Look at *me*? Look at *me*? Give him ten minutes
with a library book and he makes the bloody world end!
Call yourself a wizard?

WATERCUP: Old fool,
I call myself Sir Watercup of the Weeds!

MERLIN: *And* he gets the girl – how is *that* fair?
Why don't I remember her? Why don't I remember *him*?

MORGANA: *(To MERLIN and WATERCUP.)* Merlin, Merlin, one day
you start at the Academy, one day
you never went at all. One day you find
a girl on the forest path and fall in love.
One day you creep on either side of hedges,
Merlin and Elaine,
and perhaps you hear a crackle underfoot
but think no more of it, and go your ways
and never meet in this world. All your days
begin on the forest path,
and here they end. They leave no consequences,
no effects, except, in waking dreams
at times you recollect those other lives
and wonder what they were. Some day this sword
is hard to pull from here, it takes a nobody.

ARTHUR: I say, that *is* a dream I had.

MORGANA: Some day
a picnic blanket is a Round Table.

LANCELOT: Blimey,
Guin, are you following this?

GUIN: She talks a lot
for a toilet cleaner.

MORGANA: Some day even a humble
water cup is holy, and these men
give half their lives to find it. But today
this was the life you chose. This was the day
a boy tried out some magic.

MERLIN/WATERCUP: But I –

MORGANA: Merlin:
we nine bright girls all wear this golden crystal:
here all your days are kept.

MERLIN/WATERCUP: But he –

MORGANA: Merlin:

(Pointing.)   Crystal.

MERLIN/WATERCUP: But I –

MORGANA: Magic.

MERLIN/WATERCUP: How can –

MORGANA: Crystal.

     We threw a ring around you all, a circle
     to save you for all time, to pass your days
     and tell your tales. From time to time we visit,
     disguised as those whom you would take for granted.
     In coats and hats we watch you from the future.
     We ascertain there is no breach or gap
     by which you might escape the enchanted O
     and suffer the world out there.
     Over that line, beyond the woods – is Time,
     loss, sickness, death. All creatures there they merely
     come and go, just once, and not again.
     But you are immortal here, in a web of story.
     I've ticked the boxes and my work is done.
     Tomorrow morning all will begin again.
     You will forget what's happened, you'll be strangers
     encountered on a forest path, each day
     a different outcome. Knights of Camelot,
     drink and be glad, life is unending story.

All Camelot celebrates. LILY and the WHITE KNIGHT murmur together in Welsh.

ELAINE: It will all begin again?

WATERCUP: I don't want that,
     Elaine, I don't *want* a different outcome
     every day.

ELAINE: I don't want to forget
     everything, I don't want to forget
     anything!

WATERCUP:	I want the day we've had,
	a world where this has happened
	and only this!
ELAINE:	A day that has a night!
WATERCUP:	A night that has a morning!
ELAINE:	A morning with you there!
WATERCUP:	Another day
	we spent until it turned
	to a yesterday we shared!
ELAINE:	What can we do?
WATERCUP:	We'll go, we'll run away!
ELAINE:	What about Lily?
WATERCUP:	She's found another Lily. She's happy.
	She doesn't need me now. It's now or never.
	Nobody's watching. We're going to leave these woods,
	they must end somewhere. That's how far we're going.

They kiss, and creep away. ARTHUR signals for the WHITE KNIGHT to kneel.

ARTHUR:	Well I don't understand a word, so no change there!
	White Horseman, I do dub thee – any ideas?
LILY:	Lily.
ARTHUR:	Yes, Sir Lily, Sir Lily of what, though?

LILY points in the direction of Wales.

LILY:	Galwa fe'n Sir Lily o Gymru. [28]
ARTHUR:	What's she pointing at? Ah.
	I do dub thee Sir Lily of Those Hedges
	Over There.
LANCELOT:	Sir Lily of Those Hedges
	Over There, I'll see you in the Lists!
GAWAIN:	I'll have a crack at ye, too, ye big girl's blouse.
MORDRED:	I swear to you, I will fall from my horse one day,
	but so will you.

[28]   Call him Sir Lily of Wales.

BORS:	That's jousting in a nutshell.
LUCAN:	Wham-bam-Bedivere, goodnight and thank you.

The KNIGHTS drink. MERLIN sees LILY and the WHITE KNIGHT together.

MORGANA:	Merlin, what's the matter?
MERLIN:	It's those two. Same-sex relationships, all very well, but that's a same-*person* partnership. I know the Universe won't come to an end, but really, you have to draw the line.
MORGANA:	I spoke at length with my mother, the Ancient Sybil of the Mountains, and she says that love is love between two persons, or, sometimes, between one. Thus spoke the Sybil.
MERLIN:	So you're saying they've got a Sybil partnership.
MORGANA:	My dear, eternity's not time enough for me to find that funny.

MERLIN notices WATERCUP has gone.

MERLIN:	Where am I?
MORGANA:	In the woods.
MERLIN:	No I mean, where am I *young?* And where's my lady?

All notice WATERCUP and ELAINE are missing.

MORGANA:	I – don't know –
MERLIN:	Why would they run away? It's a happy ending.
MORGANA:	They won't get very far. As they approach the edges of the wood their memories will start to fail. They won't know one another.
ARTHUR:	Search party! Off we go! Spread out, eh!

All fan out into the woods. WATERCUP and ELAINE elsewhere.

ELAINE:	I think we were here before.
WATERCUP:	No I don't think so.
ELAINE:	We were following the sunset.

WATERCUP: No, no,
we were seeking a Tournament.

ELAINE: I don't think so,
Waterlily.

WATERCUP: Watercup.

ELAINE: What's that?

WATERCUP: I don't know, I was telling you my name,
Eleanor.

ELAINE: Emily. No, Allie. Annie.

WATERCUP: It doesn't matter.

ELAINE: What doesn't matter?

WATERCUP: Our names,
they don't matter. We'll hold hands.

ELAINE: Yes, hold hands.
Let's take it in turns to try and remember things.
I'll go first.

WATERCUP: First at what.

ELAINE: I don't know.
Just hold my hand.

WATERCUP: I'm holding your hand, Eileen.

ELAINE: What did you just call me?

WATERCUP: El – *Elaine!*

ELAINE: *Water – cup*, let's go this way, quickly,
things are coming back to me! I'm remembering
everything!

WATERCUP: It's coming back,
the Tournament, the Book, my sister Lily –
I can see the edge of the woods, I can see a light!

A bright light shines on them.

ELAINE: There's a way out of the woods!

WATERCUP: The toilet cleaner –
Morgana, she said she always ticks the boxes,
but *I ticked one of them* – she must have thought
she'd done it! There's a gap we can get out through!

ELAINE:	Watercup…
WATERCUP:	Elaine?
ELAINE:	If we stayed here, all would – begin again.
WATERCUP:	What do you mean?
ELAINE:	Here, in the woods, it would all *begin*. It would never – end. If we leave the woods, she said, out there – things – will end some day. Us. You and I. All things.
WATERCUP:	You think – you think we should turn back? Forget it all? Begin the day again? Pass on either side of hedges…
ELAINE:	Hear the crackle underfoot…
WATERCUP:	And think no more of it…
ELAINE:	And go our ways…
WATERCUP:	And never meet in this world.
ELAINE:	And you'd be a nobody again and not *my* nobody…
WATERCUP:	And there we would stay, forever…
ELAINE:	Forever telling different stories… Out there – what if there *are* no stories? Only Time, and loss and death and whatever the other one was.
WATERCUP:	What's *that* – compared to *this*? Us, forever! Till it's over.
ELAINE:	Us, forever, till it's over.
WATERCUP:	Here's my hand.
ELAINE:	Here's mine, Sir Watercup of the Weeds. Let's go where things will end some day. Let's go there now, together.

ELAINE and WATERCUP run off into the light. The HERALD comes by, and sings.

HERALD: *The Seventh of June and the Eighth of May*
Are happy together a mile away,
The Second of March and the Twelfth of July
Married in secret and I know why,
The Ninth of November will always remember
The day she set eyes on the Sixth of September
  And all that's to be
  And all that are gone
Are off to the dance with their glad-rags on

The night you arrive and the day we part
Are watching the road from the back of the cart
The moment you loved and the hour you lost
Are crossing a garden that has to be crossed
The year you were fine and the year you were mine
Are dining together where we *used to dine*
  And all that are gone
  And all that's to be
Is off to the dance with my baby and me

ARTHUR, GUINEVERE, MERLIN, MORGANA, LANCELOT, GAWAIN, MORDRED, LUCAN, BORS, THE WHITE KNIGHT and LILY dance.

  And all that's to come
  And all that are gone
Are off to the dance with their glad-rags on

WATERCUP and ELAINE, dressed like people dress today, dance with them all.

  All that are gone
  And all that's to be
Is off to the dance with my baby and me

And all bow, and all dance away.

*   *   *   *   *